You,

    Beast

Wisconsin Poetry Series

Ronald Wallace, *Series Editor*

You,
Beast

Nick Lantz

The University of Wisconsin Press

Publication of this volume has been made possible, in part, through support from the Brittingham Fund.

The University of Wisconsin Press
1930 Monroe Street, 3rd Floor
Madison, Wisconsin 53711-2059
uwpress.wisc.edu

3 Henrietta Street, Covent Garden
London WC2E 8LU, United Kingdom
eurospanbookstore.com

Printed in the United States of America

This book may be available in a digital edition.

Library of Congress Cataloging-in-Publication Data

Names: Lantz, Nick, author.
Title: You, beast / Nick Lantz.
Other titles: Wisconsin poetry series.
Description: Madison, Wisconsin : The University of Wisconsin Press, [2017]
  | Series: Wisconsin poetry series
Identifiers: LCCN 2016041567 | ISBN 9780299311742 (pbk. : alk. paper)
Subjects: LCSH: Human-animal relationships—Poetry. | LCGFT: Poetry.
Classification: LCC PS3612.A586 Y68 2017 | DDC 811/.6—dc23
LC record available at https://lccn.loc.gov/2016041567

For

Vicky

Contents

Oh, the Humanity

Fables

Acknowledgments

Several poems in this book were completed with the generous support of a faculty research grant from Sam Houston State University.

Many thanks to the journals that published some of these poems, sometimes in earlier forms and under different titles.

Blackbird
B O D Y
Construction Magazine
Copper Nickel
Gettysburg Review
jubilat
Minnesota Review
New England Review
Pleiades

The poems "Roach, Kitchen Floor," "Armadillo, I-45," and "Grackle, Walmart" are adapted from the text I wrote for "In Place," a collaborative project with the musical duo Lungta (John Lane and Amanda Pepping).

Many thanks to Shara Lessley and Cynthia Marie Hoffman for their advice on the manuscript.

Over Every Creeping Thing

Posthumanism

In the good old days, the lords
summering in the country
paid peasants to beat
the ponds all night with branches
so the frogs would stay
silent. Armstrong and Aldrin left
snow angels in moon dust.
Foxes waited patiently
around the shoulders
of the high-born ladies
drowning with the Titanic.
The emperor's clockwork
nightingale sang
only Top 40 Classic Rock.

But one evening, so many starlings
roosted on the hands
of the town clock, time stopped
for six minutes.
We should have known then.

Just last week, a moose
stopped in the middle

of Main Street. A driver
rolled down his window.
"Hey!" he shouted. "Hey!"
said a blue jay on a mailbox.
"Hey!" said a squirrel to a dog.
"Hey!" said the driver.
"Hey!" said the dog.
"Hey!" said the driver.
"Hey!" said the bees.
"Hey!" said the flower. "Hey!"

The Prisoner

In a dingy cell, Menes the stork paces, stops, turns a stone over with the tip of its beak, resumes pacing. Outside the cell, a chair and table. The jailer walks in, collapses into the chair, unfolds a newspaper.

JAILER   Have you heard, Menes, how the elections are going?

MENES   How can I know anything in here? There is no television, no window. Why don't you give me some of your paper?

The jailer hesitates.

JAILER   No, no, I don't think so.

MENES   Just the sports, friend. There's no politics in sports.

JAILER   Ach. Sports is all politics.

MENES   Yes, that's what my father always said. The funny pages then?

JAILER   They've been discontinued.

MENES   Truly?

The jailer holds up the paper. Several squares have been cut out of it.

JAILER   At the ministry, a dozen men work night and day to cut the cartoons from each issue.

MENES   Why still print them in the first place?

The jailer's voice is a distant village burning.

JAILER   Because this is a democracy, of course.

MENES   Yes, yes, true. Well, why don't you read some of it to me?

JAILER   Oh no, I can't do that.

MENES   What's the harm, friend?

JAILER   I cannot read.

The jailer shrugs, continues reading.

MENES   That is a shame. You attended the government schools?

JAILER   Yes.

MENES   They taught you how to assemble a rifle?

JAILER   Of course.

MENES   And how to enter a house at night . . .

JAILER   . . . and take those inside, yes. They must believe they are dreaming, even as you pull bags over their heads and march them to a field, they must whisper to themselves "I am still in my bed, my wife is beside me."

MENES   And when you put them in a grave in the field, the words you were taught to say?

The jailer's recitation is a groove worn in a millstone.

JAILER   "Here is your bed, brother. Your children are asleep in their rooms. Your wife lies in bed beside you."

MENES   And she does.

JAILER   Yes.

A pause so long that the dead forget that they are dead.

MENES   Perhaps I will tell you a story instead?

The jailer looks around.

JAILER   Alright then.
MENES   A boy and a stick . . .

A hundred soldiers march on stage, drag the jailer away. A shot. A different man enters, wearing the jailer's blood-spattered clothes, a false mustache.

MENES   What on earth was that?
JAILER   Elections. Do not worry.
MENES   Who are you?

As cheerful as shrapnel.

JAILER   It is I, your old friend the jailer!

Menes looks at the jailer's gun.

MENES   Ah, you've done something different with your hair?
JAILER   That must be it.

The jailer picks up the paper from the ground. Reads it upside down.

MENES   What news?

JAILER   No news. Only the funny pages. By order of the new government.

             *He shows the paper, the same bright cartoon of a building on
             fire, page after page.*

MENES   Read one to me?

JAILER   Happily. A boy and a stick . . .

             *A hundred soldiers march on stage, drag the jailer away. A
             shot. A child enters, wearing the jailer's ill-fitting clothes,
             carrying a stick. He sits down and draws a mustache on his
             lip with a black marker.*

MENES   Who are you?

             Standing on his chair.

JAILER   I am the jailer! I have always been the jailer, and I will always be the
             jailer!

MENES   The wisdom of the ages. You are a true philosopher, sir.

             *The jailer folds the paper into a helmet, puts it on his head. He
             makes his stick into a rifle, fires it at Menes.*

JAILER   Pew! Pew! Pew! I got you. Now you have to tell me a story!

MENES   Very well. Once, the frogs yearned for someone to rule over them, so they begged God to send them a king. God thought they were foolish, and threw a log into their pond, saying, "Here is your king." The frogs, frightened at first by the loud splash, hid and trembled, but when they saw the log did not move, they grew contemptuous and climbed upon it, croaking loudly, "This king is not worthy of us! Send us the king we deserve!" God heard their complaints, and sent a stork, saying, "Here is your king."

JAILER   And? What happened?

MENES   Why, the stork ate all the frogs, of course.

A hundred soldiers march on stage, carrying sticks. The sticks are rifles. A shoot-out ensues.

JAILER   Pew! Pew! Pew!

SOLDIERS   Pew! Pew! Pew!

The soldiers fall over dead, heaped in piles almost to the ceiling. A stagehand dumps buckets of blood from the catwalks. The jailer is wounded. He strips to his underwear, hands his clothes through the bars.

JAILER   You must carry on. For the sake of the republic!

The jailer dies. Menes puts on the jailer's clothes, paces the cell.

END

Armadillo, I-45

Herodotus said we cry
because we know much and control
nothing. This is just another name
for history. But the armadillo walks, head down,
across grass or asphalt just the same, each step
the indifference of history. At the store, I buy my steaks
wrapped in plastic. My fingernails are all that's left
of a long and bloody history. The armadillo's shell
has weathered feral dogs and BB guns, but the fender of a car
is hard and bright as history. Tonight, when we cut
the steak and pour our wine, we will eat
the final sentences of a history. At dusk, something ancient
leaves its burrow. Nothing is ever as close
or far away as history. When we see a body
beside the road, we look away. We never liked
to study that sort of human history.

Stallion: An Epistle

Race horse names

Dear Abby—
Ima Cowboy Yes I Am. Just Between Us, Ima Hustler Baby, Last
     Man Standing. Never Say Never.
Believe It Takes Two: Alexander the Great Cuddles Miss Congeniality.
     Diamonds 'R Us . . . Abracadabra: Little Man, Little Lady. Imagine
     That.
Paris City of Romance: Genuine Mastercard. Mid Mornings Light
     Breeze, Falling Leaves, Kodak Moment.
Just Between Us, Ain't Misbehavin. Nevertheless, Never Say Never.
It's A Long Story: Bar Room, Oh My Gosh, Barbie Geisha On High
     Heels In the Moonlight. Just a Flirt, Little Extra Credit, Bad
     Whiskey, Oblivion.
Short Story: Say It Ain't So/Jumping to Conclusions. Say It Ain't
     So/One Night Only. Say It Ain't So/Another Chance. Say It
     Ain't So/Please Baby Please. Look at Me Go/Say It Ain't So.
Good Man, If Only (Question Mark). Daggers Point, Keener Than
     Keen.
Pardon My Dust, Deal Me In, Bail Me Out, Beam Me Up Scottie,
     Redeem My Heart. Never Say Never.

Always,
Horse

P.S. I Love You

Snake Bites Orit Fox, Israeli Model, on the Breast, Later Dies of Silicone Poisoning

—headline

One kind of looking
is venomous. The other sops up
poison like a dry rag.

Photons are a million
hypodermic teeth. This Potemkin village
of a heart is propped up
by sticks in the back. A man in the wings
turns the crank that works my mouth, pumps
the bellows of my lungs with his foot.

Dear God, please shoot me
from my good side: the albedo of my teeth,
measured in lumens, measured in watts, measured
in megatons.

If you
bite me,

how can I
be the villain? If it is in your nature
to bite, in mine
to be bitten?

It's Cleopatra who says the greatest are misthought
for things others do. And she welcomed
that last kiss to her breast.

It's not true, this poisoning. Even if you could
suck the venom from me, how could it kill

you, eater of vermin, you who dissolve
fur and bone as I might

a cube of sugar on my tongue? When we fall,
we answer others' merits in our name.

My name means light, each ravenous particle
gnawing at the eye. Look at me.

Now look at you.

Are we not therefore to be pitied?

Roach, Kitchen Floor

oh to be abject
to scuttle
to lurk
to lie flat
to oar the air with antennae finer than a calligrapher's brush

oh to preface every sentence with *above*
as in, *above me a fluorescent sun quaking*
as in, *above the towering architecture of appliance*

to see the underside of the table over which others bow their heads
to breathe the darkness inside a closed cabinet

oh to tremble to the echo that fills the empty pots at night

to be six-legged
to be hard of shell and soft of flesh

oh to evade
to vanish from sight
to be a blotch in the corner of every eye

or to be crushed, poisoned, delivered
unto that terrible unknown martyrdom

Randy Johnson Fastball Kills Dove: Spring Training, March 24, 2001

A thread of space,
a blue-white arc

between two nodes.
How impossible:

the berries, protozoan
slime, footprints, transcription

errors, taut grass, yowl of primitive
gut, hands waving
over firelight—all this

formed the jaw, the lithe
tongue that forms
Impossible, no way

out of nothing
but thrumming

air, in front of a glowing box

funneling radiation
into the image

of a man bending,
turning, and—a ball

(rubber, yarn, leather)

tunneling that slim
tunnel of space-time.

To say nothing

of intersection. An archer
fires an arrow

over the castle wall
to impress a woman;

in the nearby forest,
the same arrow

pierces her father's throat
as he returns

from a long journey.

Or a building, say,
slow as the origin of species, reaches

to catch something
glittering,
something falling
from the sky

and is erased by fire.

The dove: vaporized.

The world snags
for a moment.
The ump consults

the rulebook. (Do not
say to me, *Impossible*.)

The call is "no pitch."
Everyone assumes
his former position

and begins again,
as if nothing
has happened.

Curiosity Killed the . . .

—Google search autocomplete

what should you do if your goldfish . . .
    is dying
    is constipated
    is pregnant

do dogs really . . .
    bury bones
    see in black and white
    love you

can pets . . .
    get lice
    carry bed bugs
    travel on greyhound

do dolphins . . .
    sleep
    have hair
    rape humans

will apes ever . . .
    evolve

        talk
        take over the world

can animals . . .
        be gay
        get high
        get stds
        have down syndrome
        think

will humans ever . . .
        evolve
        walk on the sun
        go extinct

what do animals think . . .
        of cars
        of music
        about death
        of us

Grackle, Walmart

If Bede's sparrow,
flitting through the mead hall's warmth
and back into the night, is the soul
returning to darkness, then what
of the grackle, who darts
through these hissing double doors
and won't come out again?

He lords high in the rafters
beyond the reach of stock boys
and their brooms. When no one
watches, he ventures down to dip
his beak in the plastic Tuscan fountain,
to glut himself on bags of waxy chips.

He lives in light that never dims.
Below him, the gawping shoppers point.
Outside, his cousins can only fill
the myrtled darkness with their noise.

Taxidermy: Gift Shop

Raccoon piloting
a canoe, coyote
in tux on hind legs
holding a tray
for champagne flutes,
trio of squirrels
bedecked in sequins
and beehive wigs
crooning one note
forever.

And you,
you turn over
the price tag
like a rare leaf.

Fishtank ↓

I got real good at running my hand through hair
I don't have anymore. There's an art to it,
like the student who wants to share his opinions
about the book he never opened, or the pilot
bombing a city whose streets he's never
walked along.
            What am I saying?
I'm the hummingbird hovering, sipping
from an open can of Diet Coke. Faith
is the kind of poison you drink to get the taste
of poison out of your mouth. My toenail
fell off this morning, but it will rise again
to a teacup full of hosannas and applause.
My surgeon says he's a magician. He waves
his hand and one of my testicles disappears.
Hell, that's nothing: I made thirty-two years
disappear without even breaking a sweat.
In the oncology waiting room, someone
taped a handwritten sign to the wall:

Fishtank ↓

And sure enough, a month later, a fish tank
appeared, the fish flashing iridescent scales,
darting, chasing after who knows what.

Snips and Snails

Drawing the Bee

The five-year-old's drawing:
distended honeybee,
fuchsia-striped,
striding long-legged
through the tiger grass,
eyes wobbly dots of wax
searching for a flower
to bury his face in.

I could say it signified
the tidy apocalypse
of divorce, the slanted light
of a therapist's office,
but that wouldn't be true.

I always drew the stars as black
knots brooding over bruises
(they might have been bears)
that tilted their heads up to gulp
at greenish air.

When I got a microscope
for my birthday, the first thing I ever trapped

on a slide was a flea
taken from the cat's neck. I drew
its delicate hairs, its needle
mouth, those legs long as a dancer's
and still twitching.

When I walked down a street,
I saw every broken
window first, followed the line
of ants to the car-struck sparrow,
heard in the train's long screech
a voice calling a name that had lost
its shape.

Now my mother sends drawings
she's found in old shoeboxes:
today, a pair of wolves on hind legs,
forepaws on each other's shoulders.
"Dancing," she says, but I know
they're strangling one another.

Toyland

Play is often talked about as if it were a relief from serious learning.
But for children play is serious learning. Play is really the work of
childhood.

—Fred Rogers

1. See 'n Say

The mother says, "I'm painting. This is my painting time."
The little sister says, "If you touch my doll again, I'll tell Mom."
The big brother says, "Get lost, faggot."
The father says, "I'll pick you up at eight, I promise."
The big brother says, "Don't tell Mom I said that."
The mother says, "You better not be breaking anything out there."
The father says, "This is M____, please leave your digits and I'll hit you right back."
The little sister says, "Where's her dress? What did you do with her dress?"
The big brother says, "Sorry, listen, just stop crying and I'll teach you how to throw
    a knife at a tree."
The mother says, "You are killing me. Just killing me, you know that?"
The knife says, *Click*.
The knife says, *Thunk*.
The father says, [What's a father again?]
The teacher says, "You're late."
The boys at school say, "Two little faggots, sittin' in a tree . . ."
Your best friend says, "I'll get my dad's gun and then we'll see. I'll fucking show them."
You? You say nothing.

2. Frogger

Keep your head down
in the hallways.
At lunch, sit at the far side
of the cafeteria.
When the stranger in front
of you on the bus,
louder each time,
keeps repeating
Hey kid, nice backpack,
look up
and shake your head,
like you don't speak
his language, like you're deaf,
like you're from another
planet. Cross
the street to avoid
the unchained dog
that barks. Cross
again before the older boys
shooting craps see you.
At your front door, wait,
listen for raised voices,
because in your favorite game, the frog,
after crossing all those lanes of traffic,
will still die
if he sets one foot inside the water,
his home.

3. Teddy Ruxpin

At ten, you'd give anything
for a different voice, to pop open
a cassette tray in your back
and slip in a new tape—that easy.

A voice that wouldn't quake or lisp.
A voice that strangers
didn't mistake for your mother's
when you picked up the phone.

So you did the next best thing:
you stole the talking bear
from your sister's room,
stole your brother's tapes
of Public Enemy, Megadeth,
replaced the bear's old voice,
and propped him on your window,
let him rant his blistering mantra
until his batteries ran down.

4. Mouse Trap

Your mother isn't drunk, exactly,
when you sit down to play.
She unpacks the pieces, her fingers
stained with paint, her hair wafting
cigarettes and gesso. She lingers
on the dregs
of wine in her mug,
trying to talk herself
out of a third pour.

Your sister is asleep.

Your brother is who-knows-where.

The mice go round the board.

You build the trap together,
but in this version of the game,
your mother gets to ask a question
each time you add a piece.
"You like that boy?" she says,
"The one who was here yesterday?"
You shrug, she rolls the dice.
It comes up six. You're under the trap.
She drains her glass, begins to turn
the crank. "Be careful," she says.

"People are always watching you."
And just like that, the cage falls.

5. Duck Hunt

The birds lurch upward over blocky grass, cathode sky.
You and your best friend take turns shooting them down
with a plastic gun. When it's his turn, you sink back
on the couch, watch him from just beyond his periphery,
the muscles of his jaw, a fuzz on his lip catching the light.
The birds fall, he hoots. When it's your turn, you miss
like always. The cartoon dog pops up from the grass, snickers
like he's laughing at more than just your lousy aim.
But your friend isn't disappointed. Though his eyes never
leave the screen, he slides forward, takes your hand in his,
says, "Hold it sideways, like this." You hold your breath.
"You can shoot the dog," he says. "Here, let me show you."

6. Puppy Surprise

It was your sister's toy, the flap
on its belly hiding a litter
of stuffed puppies, which disappeared, one by one,
in the weeks after Christmas.
Your sister cried over the loss, but that
was OK. When she crammed the puppies
back in, pulled them out,
fished her little arm
elbow deep into its empty body,
you had to look away.
She discarded
the barren dog,
but your mother adopted it,
started stashing her watch
and credit cards in its empty womb,
until your brother found
that hiding place too.
Then it lived under
the back window
of his beat-up Civic,
muling baggies of weed.
He strutted around the park
with it under his arm,
made a big show of doting
on it in front of girls,
till a couple of guys

grabbed it and ran.
You found him on the front step,
and he said, "They took my dog,"
and you started crying,
and instead of punching you
he started crying too,
put his arm around you,
and you both cried about it
like it was a real dog.

7. Hungry Hungry Hippos

Your big brother is always hungry, chews
his fingers to the quick, stands
at the open fridge, irradiated by its light.

His friends are hungry too. They come over
when Mom isn't home
and work the house like sharks
working the floating carcass of a whale.

They're hungry for your VHS tapes
and Nintendo cartridges, for the silverware
and the pill bottles on Mom's dresser
and the chemicals under the sink.

They open up all the board game boxes
and take the dice.

They leave your mother's paintings,
but pocket the tubes of paint.

They run their hands
through the couch, slow,
like each cushion
is the body of a lover.

You have a coin from Germany,
and some car stickers,

so you stuff them in a Safeway bag
and toss them out the window.

Then your brother's friends come around
and shake you down.
What you got? What you got?

When they leave, your brother makes himself
a cheese and mustard sandwich.
When Mom's car pulls up,
he runs out the back.

8. The Oregon Trail

At school, in the computer lab, you learn
about American history. The oxen, the rattlesnakes,
the buffalo that collapse like a building when shot,
how no matter what provisions the pioneers buy
before setting out in their blocky Conestoga,
Billy dies of dysentery, or Suzy drowns
while fording the digital river. You never
get them to Oregon before the period is over.
Each time, you leave your party stranded,
a trail of loss strung behind them,
graves dug in the hard prairie soil,
too far out to turn back.

9. Barrel of Monkeys

You once overheard your mother on the phone
joking that she rents a house
in the worst neighborhood of the best school district.

Your sister has learned how to accept
gifts from your father with just the right mixture
of gratitude and disappointment
so that he will buy her anything she asks for.

Your father, in turn, has trained your sister
to deliver his postdated checks
after his car is already blocks away.

Your brother knows just how much he can steal
from your mother before she will change
the locks, and just how long he has to wait

before she will give him the new key.

You sit on the floor of your bedroom,
lowering a plastic monkey
into a pile of identical monkeys,
so that one links hands
with another, which in turn grabs another,
until you have them all dangling,
arm in arm,
a single tenuous chain.

10. Piñata

Blindfolded, spun, you can be forgiven
your misses, the hollow whoosh
as stick cuts air. And maybe your father, late
on his last check, can be forgiven
for pulling up to the curb
and handing you an unwrapped toy
through his open window.
And your best friend, eating his plate of cake:
you can forgive him,
in the presence of these other boys,
for standing a little farther
away from you. And who can blame
those other boys
for not saying much? You invited them
because you could rely on them
not to say anything about your house
next week at school.
You'll forgive your mother, too,
for hanging the cardboard burro so high
in the yard's one slouching tree,
for cinching the blindfold so tightly,
for grabbing your shoulders and spinning you
till you can barely stand.
You can forgive anything
when the stick makes contact,
when you hear something break,
and you swing and swing and swing.

Taxidermy:
Bobcat Leaping after Pheasant

In the photo of your brother, he's just thrown a ball
from the far side of the field, its white dot barely visible
at the top of the frame. But it will never descend
to where you crouch in the foreground, fist in mitt,
waiting, in 1985. That mitt is outgrown
and sold, that ball lost
to the blackberry bushes
of another summer day, that brother
gone. You know what it is to be arrested forever
midleap, midflight, as if your claws
might just close around your desire,
as if you might just escape this time
unscathed. And who remembers now
if the ball ever found your glove?

Natasha

Oh darlink, oh darlink, won't you give up
moose and squirrel business? I am in kitchen
sharpenink knives, I am in bedroom sharpenink
myself, but you sit on couch, you watch on TV
moose pull America out of hat, recite *I wandered*
lonely as cloud. Daffodils I do not want,
my darlink. I want to be nogoodnik with you,
and you alone. Squirrel sounds like MiG plane
but laughs like Boy Scout, and every time,
it is your face bomb explodes in, you and I
left holdink bag. Won't you come outside,
see cloud that looks like anvil about to drop
on neighbors? I have recipe for happiness,
and it is this: forget blueprints, rubber masks,
bombs like big black cherries. Forget even
Fearless Leader and his dusty monocle.
Let us go then, you and I, and I will show you
all of dead baby birds left behind in nests,
show you prisons, tent cities, oil slicks
big as heartland. Just give me chance, my darlink,
and I will show you sometink you will really like.

Oh, the Humanity

NO ILLEAGLES HERE

—spray painted on the side of a building

What to do with the sickly eagles, brooding
in their brownstones and double-wides?
They learned compassion from the fox
that flees the henhouse with bloody lips,
so how can they be expected to feel
what the fish feels when it's swept
from the river in their bright claws?

On TV, one proud bird complains
of crows that mob him on the street.
History is history. Right is right. So what
if his father, and his father's father et al.,
raided their nests, killed their young?

After all, he teaches his sons to say
please and thank you, how to change
their own oil, how to pull up their pants,
how to cradle the butt
of a Bushmaster M4 Carbine
against the shoulder, how to stand
their ground. He bows his sharp beak
over the supper table, speaks words

soft as eider down. He votes
his conscience, has heart-to-hearts
with his god. He sees what the world
is coming to. On his weekends
he paces the capitol lawn,
holding his handmade sign:
IF YOUR NOT OUTRAGED
YOUR NOT PAYING ATTENTION.

Polar Bear Attacks Woman . . .
Horrifying Vid (Click to Watch)

My students and I are discussing the mediatization of 9/11 in contemporary poetry, how hardly any poems look directly at an event itself—say, planes striking the towers—but instead look only at representations of the event, footage to be paused, replayed. *Is this a failure of courage*, I ask, *this inability to look?*

One of them brings up Magritte's painting of a pipe that is not a pipe but a painting of one. *This is not a pipe*, it says, in French.

Or maybe we simply can't bear to look. *Stare directly at a solar eclipse*, our teachers always said, *and you'll go blind.* So we built boxes, tiny rooms with only a pinhole through which the eclipse could enter and be contained.

In a movie, a sixty-foot monster attacks New York. The hero's friends are eaten, crushed. His girlfriend is impaled on rebar. The city burns. We witness all this through the hero's camcorder, which continues recording even after his death. We believe in this monster not because of its enormity, not because of any measure of human suffering, but because the camera shakes, cuts out. We believe in distortion, static. The camera does not belong to the hero. The camera is the hero.

Apparently all movies in which buildings are destroyed are now actually about 9/11. But sometimes a cigar is just a cigar. Sometimes a burning building is just a burning building. Except when it is a video of a burning building. *Ceci n'est pas un bâtiment en feu.*

I enjoy watching videos in which captive animals attack their handlers without warning. A horse kicks a man. An ape on a talk show grabs the host by the neck and shakes. *Enjoy* is perhaps the wrong word. The sudden acts of violence in these videos feel valuable. I turn each one over in my mind, an aphorism to be considered.

A goose chases a crying toddler around a petting zoo enclosure.

A circus elephant stomps on its handler's head.

Years ago, I watch a video: a woman being attacked by a polar bear at the zoo. The bear has stuck its head through the bars of its cage. It grips the woman's thigh in its mouth, tries to pull her through the gap in the bars. Two men run to the woman's aid, striking the bear on the face with flimsy branches. The bear does not seem to notice. And every time—every time—I forget for a moment that someone is still standing there, filming the whole thing.

The polar bear's name is Binky. (*Ceci n'est pas un ours.*)

The title of the video is something like "Polar Bear Attacks Woman . . . Horrifying Vid (Click to Watch)." And I do—I click to watch.

I know someone who likes to point out that he does not own a television. I do not point out how much time he spends watching videos on his cell phone, hunched over the warm screen as if it is an orphaned bird he is feeding with his attention.

On my walk to work this morning, I stop to watch two roosters dueling in the middle of the street. Cars slow to pass around them as they lunge and jab at one another with their spurs. The moment I take out my phone to start filming them, the roosters break apart, the dispute forgotten, and begin pecking at the asphalt. This strikes me as the animal equivalent of putting one's hands in one's pockets and whistling. The force of my disappointment surprises me, that I have failed to capture this bit of violence on film, that I would want to possess such a thing on film.

On May 6, 1937, the *Hindenburg* zeppelin bursts into flames above an airfield in New Jersey. It is one of the first disasters caught on film. A recorded radio broadcast captures the reaction of Herbert Morrison in the moments of the crash:

It's starting to rain again; it's—the rain has slacked up a little bit. The back motors of the ship are just holding it just, just enough to keep it from—It burst into flames! Get this, Charlie! Get this, Charlie! It's fire—and it's crashing! It's crashing terrible! Oh, my, get out of the way, please! It's burning and bursting into flames, and the— and it's falling on the mooring-mast and all the folks agree that this is terrible, this is one of the worst catastrophes in the world. [unintelligible] It's–it's—it's the flames, [unintelligible] oh, four- or five-hundred feet into the sky and it . . . it's a terrific crash, ladies and gentlemen. It's smoke, and it's flames now . . . and the frame is crashing to the ground, not quite to the mooring-mast. Oh, the humanity, and all the passengers screaming around here. I told you, I can't even talk to people whose friends are on there. Ah! It's—it's—it's—it's . . . oh! I—I can't talk, ladies and gentlemen. Honest, it's just laying there, a mass of smoking wreckage. Ah! And everybody can hardly breathe and talk, and the screaming. Lady, I—I'm sorry. Honest: I—I can hardly breathe. I—I'm going to step inside where I cannot see it. Charlie, that's terrible. Ah, ah—I can't. I, listen, folks, I—I'm gonna have to stop for a minute because I've lost my voice. This is the worst thing I've ever witnessed.

No one filmed this, but here you can watch me weeping in my closed office as I watch an online video of campus police striking former U.S. Poet Laureate Robert Hass with a baton. Hass is protesting something. War, budget cuts—that's not my point. He is standing shoulder to shoulder with other protesters. He is angry, but he is also a seventy-something poetry professor in Berkeley, California. He probably shops at Whole Foods. And the police officer is hitting him with a baton. But this is not what made me begin to weep. It was an earlier clip of another protest on the same campus, an officer grabbing a biology professor, Celeste Langan, by her hair and throwing her, face-first, onto the ground.

I say to my students, *I have never seen the planes striking the towers. Not ever.* But while this is true, it is also obvious. On the morning of September 11, 2001, I was a college student in Portland, Oregon, getting ready for class. What I mean is that I have not seen any footage of planes striking the towers. And I haven't. Not ever.

This is the worst thing I've ever witnessed. (This is the worst thing I've ever not witnessed.)

At the time of the attack, Binky lives at the Alaska Zoo. The Alaskan state flag contains several of the stars that form the constellation Ursa Major, the great bear.

I watch Russian dashboard camera videos. This is a genre. Apparently many people in Russia mount cameras in their cars, to protect them from insurance fraud and corrupt police. But I like to imagine it is also because these Russians understand how disaster and mayhem are sitting just beyond the horizon's threshold. From the dashboards of the Russians, I see eighteen-wheelers crumple and roll, see moose stumble drunkenly into traffic, see a motorist beaten by men in animal costumes, explosions, babushkas tottering across the expressways.

Much of what makes violence feel violent is its proportionality, or lack thereof. In a video game, everything tries to kill you. Water can kill you. A single pixel can puncture your heart. So you kill everything that moves, and this feels as natural as breathing. Langan, the biology professor, is just standing there. Her only violence, if it can be called that, is refusing to move.

As a child, in California, I watch the Rodney King beating on the news. Or, rather, footage of the beating. I watch footage of the riots, LA on fire. This is a year after the Oakland Hills fire fills my neighborhood with smoke; three years after the Loma Prieta earthquake collapses freeways a few miles from my house. To me, the riots, the burning city on TV, are not consequences of a specific act of violence, but rather natural disasters.

In my favorite video game, when a mercenary won't give me information I want, I push him out of a high-rise window. His only crime, that I know of, is his refusal to acquiesce to my demands. He is wearing a helmet that hides his face, and his fellow mercenaries were just shooting at me. So I do not hesitate. It is fun to watch him fall.

More than a decade after 9/11, I see the photo of the Falling Man for the first time: the North Tower behind his suspended body, his posture almost relaxed. I did not intend to see the photo, did not want to see it, but it appeared, a thumbnail at the top of an Internet search, and I clicked on it.

Oh, the humanity. Which is to say, seeing another human being as a human being is always painful. And the mind refuses.

Daryl Gates, former Los Angeles chief of police: *I will be the first one to tell you that, when you see somebody being hit with a baton, it is repulsive. It repels me.*

And it as if I can almost hear him saying *But. Except. Although. However. And yet . . .*

I play a lot of video games. In my favorite video game, my character must make several ethical choices, which is to say, I must make several ethical choices on behalf of my character, through my character. My character (I) must resolve the dispute between a group of space aliens and the robots that evicted them from their home planet three hundred years earlier. The aliens wear masks that cover their faces; their women wear a sort of hijab. They have Middle Eastern accents. They live in a diaspora of spaceships, without a planet, praying for the restoration of their homeland. I find the muddy historical parallels of all this characterization troubling, but I still enjoy the game.

Camera means room. The earliest camera was a darkened room with a hole in its wall. *Camera obscura.* An empty room.

I should also mention that the woman at the zoo—the video's narrator says her name is Kathryn—climbed over two barriers in the hopes of getting a better photo of Binky. Watching her fight as Binky struggles to pull her through the bars, I feel only the dimmest compassion for her. Though I can imagine myself into her body, I cannot imagine myself into her situation, because I cannot imagine myself climbing over the two barriers separating me from Binky the polar bear. My imagination—which does not refuse even Binky's teeth puncturing the flesh of my thigh, tearing muscle as he thrashes his head—refuses this choice.

Ceci n'est pas un choix.

I should also mention that the aliens created the robots as slaves, and the robots rebelled. So the aliens tried to kill them. That is why the robots chased the aliens

54

away from their home world. The situation is meant, I think, to evoke ambivalence. The aliens are homeless, desperate, and openly discriminated against by other races. But they refuse to accept responsibility for the enslavement and attempted genocide of the robots.

I am trying to imagine my way into the mind of a police officer who hits a poet with a baton, a police officer who grabs a biology professor by the hair and throws her against the ground. The thought-armor with which he must dress his mind in order to put on his uniform, drive to the UC Berkeley campus, and hurt people simply for standing where they are not wanted. The mind refuses.

I'm going to step inside where I cannot see it.

Binky has his own Wikipedia page. His picture shows him with Kathryn's shoe in his mouth.

Robot means *slave* or *serf*. The word as we know it comes from the 1920 Czech play *R.U.R.* In my favorite video game, the robots are called *synthetics*. In one of my favorite movies, a robot says he prefers the term *synthetic person*. This movie is from 1986, and this bit of dialogue is a cynical, Reaganite-era jab at so-called political correctness. (*Political correctness* is what someone calls treating people with respect when he doesn't believe those people deserve respect.) I find this moment in the film troubling, bothersome, unfunny. But I love the film. At its climax, the heroine climbs inside a mechanical forklift suit and gets in a boxing match with a giant alien monster.

A few years after beginning this essay, I return to add this: On the streets of New York, a police officer chokes to death a man, Eric Garner, for selling loose cigarettes. A bystander captures the whole thing on video.

I can hardly breathe. (But I can breathe.)

I go back to what I wrote about Hass when I began this essay: *He probably shops at Whole Foods.* What do I mean by that, exactly? That he is middle class, respectable, nonthreatening? That he does not have an arrest record, that he is not the sort of person who deserves being harassed by police? That he is white? This thought troubles me, so I cut the sentence.

Toward the end of my favorite video game, I reconcile the aliens and the robots, broker a treaty. But I choose this option because it is the most expedient way to get both the aliens and the robots to assist me in my own mission. Honestly, I think the aliens deserve to wander homeless forever, perhaps to die off. For their stubbornness, for their unwillingness to imagine their way into the minds of others. This vindictiveness troubles me (see: the muddy historical parallels mentioned earlier).

I reinsert the sentence *He probably shops at Whole Foods*. No, I did not mean that Hass is white, exactly, rather that I could easily imagine myself in his position, though that is perhaps the same thing. Hass is angered, probably bruised, but he can go home and write a poem about it. Garner is dead. Garner probably did not shop at Whole Foods. I'm faced with the possibility that what makes violence feel violent is not proportionality at all, but the capacity to imagine yourself into the mind and body of another person. The more I think about what I have failed to imagine, what I fail to imagine on a daily basis, the sicker I feel.

Daryl Gates, again: *No one knew what Rodney King had done beforehand to be stopped. No one realized that he was a parolee and that he was violating his parole. No one knew any of those things. All they saw was this grainy film and police officers hitting him over the head.*

In the time between the afternoon I sit in my office watching as Hass is struck by police and the afternoon that I write this paragraph, over three dozen unarmed black people have been killed by police. I find the list online. Or, rather, I find a list that goes back twenty-five years, and I count out the deaths that have occurred in the three years I've been writing this essay. Most of their names are unfamiliar to me. Garner's death just happens to have been caught on tape.

When I begin revising this essay, I search online for the original video of the polar bear attacking the woman. At first, I cannot find it. It turns out there are many videos of different polar bears attacking different women. I watch them all.

The title of the Binky video has changed. The footage has been edited and repackaged as part of a clip show about animal attacks. This time, as I rewatch it, I listen to the bystanders. *Can somebody call someone?* a woman says. The narrator of the video says that Kathryn was *hoping to get a close-up photo of Binky in his cage. Instead, Binky got the close-up.*

I'm gonna have to stop for a minute because I've lost my voice.

I have also been watching online recordings of video game play. This is also a genre. The maker of one of these recordings chats casually about his commute to work, his horrible boss, as his digital avatar rounds the corner of a postapocalyptic city and shoots another player's avatar in the back of the head with a sawed-off shotgun. The digital head explodes in a convincing shower of blood that leaves momentary digital flecks on the lens of a camera that does not actually exist. Digital smoke rises from the gaping chamber of the gun. The player says how impressed he is with these game mechanics, the precise sound of the breach popping open, snapping closed again.

Ceci n'est pas une mort.

Almost exactly a year after attacking Kathryn, Binky dies. Mourners leave bouquets of flowers at the zoo.

The fact that we now capture every public tragedy on a hundred shaky camera phone videos means that these tragedies will remain forever a raw wound. Or it means these catastrophes will never be real to us. Such suffering is a dead and distant star whose light will continue to stream down on us for thousands of years. The Falling Man will never become the Man Who Fell—he will always be falling.

But there is also this. On February 15, 2013, near dawn, a meteor passes above Chelyabinsk, Russia. Because of the Russian dashboard cameras, this event, only a few seconds long, is captured over a dozen times, from a dozen different angles. Watching, I see night become, for a moment, day. I hear the garbled exclamations in Russian that I do not need to understand in order to understand.

To see something fall burning from the sky, *a terrific crash.*

Ceci n'est pas un météore. Yes, yes, however: this not-meteor—pixelated, trembling—is one of the most beautiful things I have not actually seen, the best thing I've ever not witnessed.

When I was teenager on a visit to Washington, DC, I stood in front of the Vietnam Veterans Memorial, bored out of my mind. I did not even take a photograph, though earlier that day I had photographed my hotel room, my lunch of Maryland crab cakes. The memorial was just stone, names, nothing.

A year later, I read Yusef Komunyakaa's poem "Facing It" for the first time. Looking into the polished surface of the Vietnam Veterans Memorial, Komunyakaa sees many things: a plane, a mother and child, a bright red bird. That is to say, he does not see these things but rather their reflected images. Toward the end of the poem, he writes: "A white vet's image floats / closer to me, then his pale eyes / look through mine." Though these two men can never occupy the same space, the same body, the same mind, their reflections can. The wall is not the war, and the poem is not even the wall, but in its lines, a mind opens, and I can step through, see what I did not see in the presence of the object itself.

So I am trying to imagine myself into the mind of Kathryn, now twenty years after the attack, at her home. I imagine forgetting, for most of the day, what happened. Then I imagine undressing at night, sitting on the edge of my bed in a dark room, tracing with my finger the constellation of old puncture wounds on my thigh. I imagine taking photos at the zoo all those years ago, looking through my camera's viewfinder at the bear's strange, inscrutable face, its yellowed fur and dark nose. I imagine climbing the barrier around the enclosure, my hands on the metal rail as I hoist the weight of my body over. Then crossing the second barrier as I draw closer to the bear, as it approaches the bars of its cage.

Based on True Events

So a dolphin gets caught
in a crab trap, then is rescued
and rehabilitated, but loses
his tail, or just the flukes,
and is going to die probably
of heartbreak, but some kid
falls in love with him (or her?),
and the dolphin eats fish
from the kid's hand, music
swells, and the dolphin
is fitted with a prosthetic
tail and learns to do tricks
for the amputated soldiers
returning from a desert
(how can a dolphin
ever imagine a desert?),
and the soldiers say
what a huge inspiration
this dolphin is, so someone
makes a movie in which
all the above occurs
and in which the dolphin

will play itself (God, the name
they've given it: Queenie,
or Felicity or something)
and the movie title is a pun
about the dolphin's tail,
its missing tail that was lost
in some asshole's crab trap,
and everyone is crying
tears of joy as the dolphin
cavorts in the 60 × 60 tank
that will be its home
until it dies, and the dolphin
squeaks and jerks
its head, and who knows
what it's trying to say.

Was I Ever Wont to Do So unto Thee?

On the subway, the wing-broken pigeon
hides under a discarded newspaper.

An elephant painting at an easel in the park
covers his face with a great, floppy ear.

The parrot climbs the water tower
and pulls out the last of her feathers,
chanting *Pretty girl, pretty girl*.

The rat drags the sprung trap
clattering down the middle
of the sidewalk so that we
must step aside.

From under a boot
the roach starts singing.
The frog in the pan
kicks hot oil
onto our shirts.

But the blind dog
looks right at
us.

Porcine

Their hearts are so like our own.
Our skin and theirs, interchangeable.
They too like to smoke and watch TV.

Their sense of taste
is more evolved than ours,
but their snouts
are mere nubs.

They too understand
that what they see
in a mirror is real,
but they spend much time
absorbed in their own reflections.

In the womb
for a brief time
they are nearly
indistinguishable from us.

Our young have even suckled
at their breasts.

In fact, their flesh is so similar to our own
that when they eat us
undercooked, our parasites
pass from our bodies
to theirs
without knowing the difference.

Mutton

A dark strip club—oh how dark. The low stage thrusts out. At its end, a vertical pole. And wolves. Wolves at the bar, wolves in dark suits at the heart-shaped tables. Garish music: techno, electronic drumbeat like tooth on bone amplified. Too loud to think. The wolves drink. The wolves talk in underwater voices. Now and then a laugh like a puncture wound. Over crackly speakers, an announcer, his enthusiasm practiced, a barbed fishhook.

ANNOUNCER   All right, fellas, the moment you've been waiting for. Making her debut at Mutton tonight . . . Little Avery!

Music changes, quieter, more of a slow thump now, someone locked in a trunk, kicking. Light the color of viscera. Little Avery, a ewe, enters. A few disinterested glances tossed her way. She holds a pair of electric shears, trailing a long extension cord. Once on stage, she dances (gyrating, rubbing up against the pole, etc.).

ANNOUNCER   Come on! Let's see it! Don't you boys want to see it? (*etc., ad lib*)

After a hesitation, Avery switches on the electric shears, their hornet whine clear over the music. A few wolves glance up, then go back to their drinks. Avery begins to shave the wool off her body, small patches at a time. A lone dollar bill lands on the stage, like a disinterested housefly. Nothing more. She continues.

ANNOUNCER   Oh yes! Fellas, ain't she a sweet young thing? *(etc., ad lib)*

A wolf rises, crosses, Avery watching. He passes the stage, passes her, goes to the buffet, fills up a plate with hot wings, returns to his seat.

ANNOUNCER   Here we go, boys! This is it! *(etc., ad lib)*

Avery finishes shaving. Everything is gone. The shears stop whining. Someone looks up, coughs. The song turns over like a bad dream. Avery retrieves the single bill, exits.

END

Balloon Animals

At sunset, balloon man walks balloon dog
through the subdivision of balloon homes.
Balloon clouds turn rosy, as at the end
of its balloon leash, balloon dog
does its balloon business on the balloon lawn.
All seems as it has been and will ever be,
but in the fading light, something glints
by the balloon curb: a tack, its point a ledge
balloon man can't help peering
over. He's never seen something so . . .
well, he has no word
for it, so he makes one: *sharp*.
He balances that word on his balloon tongue
as he lifts the thing, carries it home,
balloon dog trotting along behind.

In the darkness of his balloon house,
staring at that point, he feels the thinness
of his skin, how the taut air inside him
longs to get out. He brings it close,
almost presses it to his balloon chest,
but just then balloon dog whimpers,
rubs its tender, knotted nose against his hand.

Taxidermy:
Fox with Dead Chicken

A crime is a crime, but sometimes
after the hanging
they prop you up in the square
and everyone takes photos.

Fables

Taxidermy:
Rabbit School, 1888

—after Walter Potter

It takes all four maps on the wall to contain
Her Majesty's Realm, its warren of colonies.
The students, forty stuffed rabbits, sit
at eternal attention, bent over tiny slates,
studious as only the dead can be.

The lesson is Geology, the grind
of continent on continent. The lesson
is History, a lion dragging itself
into the desert to die. The lesson
is Astronomy, the frothy outer edges
of the Milky Way like a wave lapping
at a distant shore and then, spent,
falling back on itself.

But not even the best pupil, his long ears
turned heavenward, can hear the sound
of an empire dying above the silence
of his missing heartbeat.

The Ass in the Lion's Skin

Oho, my friend, it's you, is it? I, too, should have been afraid if I hadn't
heard your voice.

—Aesop

At breakfast a servant cuts the crust
from our toast
and then must swallow
the knife and fork while we watch.

Let the other barnyard beasts bark and crow
at one another. We learned long ago
to let our claws and dollars do the talking.

Our statue in the city square
is handsome in its silence: spectacles, mustache, leonine hair,
one arm outstretched, pointing to the future.

Over that arm, we have thrown a hundred nooses.

Lions Are Fed Donkeys
in Baghdad Zoo: YouTube

Shall I transcribe what I heard? A voice, the gasp
of a prosthetic knee. Grass taken into the mouths
of two donkeys [*They have no clue what's going on.*] grazing
behind a fence; behind another, people screaming.
        No, not the right word: jeering.
The difference between fear and derision thin
as the blood-brain barrier.

        Mortality displacement.
That's what the general said, microphones
        [*You're gonna die, bitch.*]
turned like flowers to the sunshine of his voice.

Balaam beat his donkey about its ears until it turned
to him and spoke: [*Ah. Ah. Ah. Ah. Ah. Ah. Ah. This
is the History Channel.*] "You have no clue, do you?"

Straightens tie, turns from microphones,
and coughs into fist, meaning: "My soul is among lions;
I lie among the sons of men Who are set on fire,

Whose teeth are spears and arrows, And their tongue
[*Eat it. Eat.*] a sharp sword."

If I hadn't heard your voice, I wouldn't know
it was you. Wind in the cyclone
fence, arrhythmia of mortar fire.
      At five minutes, thirty-one seconds
[*Open that cage—I only got four minutes left.*]
one still kicks at the wet, toothy faces. Fingers hooked
in the chain link. [*He's got blood all over his face.*]
Sometimes I don't know what they're shouting.
[*I wanna see that big one.*]
      It may be another language.

Read the names, make a tally. A check box for missing
/left leg, below knee/
/right leg, below knee/
/left leg, above knee/
/right leg, above knee/
[*Those guys are looking around, breathing.*]

If you cracked open the carcass
of this country, would honey
[*Go ahead, eat up.*] flow out?

"The roaring of the lion, The voice
of the fierce lion, And the teeth
of the young lions are broken."
    Which is to say: "500 major

amputations—toes and fingers
aren't counted." Do the math.

Nine lions. Two donkeys. One
doesn't even run. I've never screamed
[*Ah, this is gonna be fucking crazy.*]
at anyone. Can you believe that?

Electrocuted in the shower (faulty wiring).
Electrocuted in a swimming pool (faulty wiring).
Sniper bullet entered behind left ear, exited
through mouth, severing [*He's about to rip
that fucking head off.*] soft palate and tongue.

All this time, the angel
of the Lord standing
in our path with his sword raised.
The general [*Look at the face on that one.*] steps up
to the microphones, teethes his bright smile.

Or the man at the bar, into his glass: "My heritage
is to me like a lion in the forest;
It cries out against me;
        Therefore I have hated it."

What do people scream about, anyway?

Sometimes, you see, they load down a donkey
with explosives, bags of broken glass, and point him

[Damn, I was kinda hoping they'd die quicker.]
toward the nearest checkpoint.

The Two Pots

"For that," he said, "is just what I am most afraid of. One touch from
you and I should be broken in pieces."

—Aesop

At the Henry Vilas Zoo, put your face through
the cutout where the orangutan's
face should be. These are my two long arms.
The thumb touches the middle finger
lightly just so. My voice is a forest
of voices in the forest. I'm learning the ancient art
of staring the plastic fronds
into flame. If only I could
speak, I'd say
I told you so.

Now, smile.

If a Lion Could Speak

If a lion could speak, we could not understand him.

—Wittgenstein

In the schoolyard, Lion played too rough. All the little boys in tatters. Muzzle bloodied. What to do? Lion wrapped his great paws in bed sheets, taped them up. Filed his teeth to nubs. By high school, he was crushing pills to snort before art class. When Lion spoke, the teachers covered their ears. Then he was gone. Signed up, shipped out. Those first days in the desert, he felt his spine grow loose. They gave him a rifle, took it back. He was a gunner, rode up top, squinting at every convoy. A sniper took his lower jaw, the left side of his face. Back home, he beat his girlfriend stupid, knocked her up. Crashed his Civic on the ice that blew in out of season. He's still sitting in his darkened den, fishing bits of glass from his face, talking to himself.

The Boy and the Snails

You abandoned creatures, how can you find heart to whistle when
your houses are burning?

—Aesop

If you are born
with the wrong number
of legs, if your heart

hangs like a pendant
outside your ribs,
if yr vwls r mssng,

if even the German shepherd trained
to rip the throats
from enemy combatants

won't so much as growl
at you, if hurricanes
joblessness carcinoma prank phone calls

well, then, what?

The Soldier and the Lion

*A soldier sits astride a lion. They traverse mountain ranges,
vacant shopping malls, the naked ocean floor. A prerecorded
voice issues from the lion's mouth.*

LION   There, through the motel window, you can see that man cheating
on his wife. When she finds out, she'll have too much to drink and
go for a drive, hit a little boy. In the hospital, doctors discover the
boy has a brain tumor, and they save his life.

SOLDIER   Mmm.

LION   Look to your left—the oil tanker bleeding into the sea. All
the people coming together on the beach to scrub the
blackened pelicans. How hopeful they are. Listen, they're
singing.

The soldier grips his rifle, grimaces.

SOLDIER   Are you sure?

LION   Yes, yes. Here, smell the grass that's grown over Gettysburg! Without
the war, there can be no treaty. No important speech. No happy
tourists picnicking by the monuments. What next? Let's stop here
for a moment.

*They stop in a hospital room. The susurrus of machinery fills
everything.*

SOLDIER   What's this?
LION   In the bed, he's dying. His organs are shutting down, like someone
            walking through the rooms of a house, turning off lights. His lover—
            there, sleeping in the chair by the window—will write lines of poetry
            about this moment, and those poems will change hundreds of lives.
SOLDIER   It doesn't seem right.

            The lion prowls onward, through factory floors, past pyramids
            swallowed by jungle.

LION   Right? What is, is right.

            They continue for years in silence, until there is only desert. The
            lion stops.

SOLDIER   I don't . . .
LION   Too bad.

            The soldier climbs down and sits on the sand. The lion sprawls
            out close by. The soldier breaks down his rifle. Lays each piece
            before the lion, who gobbles it up. Then the rifle is gone.

LION   More.

            The soldier takes off his armor. The lion eats it.

LION   More.

            The soldier looks around. Finds nothing. He takes off his clothes.
            He is naked. The lion eats his clothes.

LION   More.

              The soldier stands.

SOLDIER   What else?

              The lion shrugs.

LION   I don't know. But more.
SOLDIER   Couldn't I just . . .

              He goes to leave.

LION   No. More.

              *The soldier sits on the rock and weeps. Slowly, he removes his
              foot. Gives it to the lion. Who swallows it whole.*

LION   Keep going.

              *Still weeping, the soldier takes apart his legs. And feeds them to
              the lion. He takes off his genitals and gives them to the lion. His
              ears and his nose. First the fingers of his left hand and then the
              whole arm.*

SOLDIER   Enough?
LION   No, more.
SOLDIER   I was sitting in my car in Ann Arbor, at a red light. Rain like boot
              heels. Forty days of it. All the gutters flooded. I'd idled at the light

for years, hours maybe. A policeman standing in the intersection, stopping traffic. I picked all the rubber off the steering wheel, picked it down to glittery bone. Forgot what my living room looked like. Soot where the policeman's face should be. Then from behind a building, an elephant, and a man leading it by a chain. The elephant walked down the middle of the street. Being led somewhere. I don't know where. It didn't look at me. It passed the intersection and I couldn't see it anymore. The policeman waved me through.

LION   Did you ever find out why it was there?
SOLDIER   I meant to, but by the time I got home, I'd forgotten about it. Can you believe that?

The lion looks him up and down.

LION   About you? Yes.

The soldier waits a moment.

SOLDIER   That too?
LION   Even that.

The soldier opens his chest like a cabinet door and reaches inside. He pulls out postcards. Utensils. A shoe. A license plate. A length of rope. A dirty magazine. Cigarette after cigarette. A handful of gleaming white beach sand. Two wedding rings. A sleeping infant. This last he holds for a moment before giving it to the lion. The lion eats. Waits. A moment passes.

SOLDIER   Who are you?

LION   Me? I'm nobody.

                The soldier casts about with his remaining hand.

SOLDIER   You seen my wallet? Something in there, I know it. Something.

                The lion rises. Stretches. Leaves. The soldier calls after it.

SOLDIER   If you see it, you'll let me know?

                *He looks around. Picks up some sand, lets it fall. He looks
                around.*

                END

The Wolf and the Crane

You can go about boasting that you once put your head into a wolf's mouth and didn't get it bitten off. What more do you want?

—Aesop

Dear X,
Been looking down
America's throat today, all wrecked
chicken bone bicycles,
watered-down cola rivers—here and there
a clot of snow, lymph clinging
to the highway shoulder.
Floodplains dotted w/ silos.
Great prophet wheel of forest fires,
in the middle a mansion
like an eye. That's what I said.
That's what I said. Aren't you
listening? Love,

From Tail to the Tooth

—a found poem

We are, as they say, tangled
in our anchor chain.

[*Laughter.*] You think
I'm kidding. [*Laughs.*] [*Laughter.*]

Ours is a nation born of ideas
and raised on improbability

from bureaucracy to the battlefield,
from tail to the tooth.

Consider this snapshot.

The man and the boy were walking
down the street with the donkey
and people looked and laughed at them and said,
"Isn't that foolish—they have a donkey
and no one rides it." So the man said
to the boy, "Get on the donkey;
we don't want those people to think
we're foolish." So they went down the road
and people looked at the boy on the donkey
and the man walking alongside—
"Isn't that terrible, that young boy
is riding the donkey and the man's walking."
So they changed places, went down the road,

people looked and said, "Isn't that terrible,
that strong man is up there on the donkey
and making the little boy walk." So they both
got up on the donkey, the donkey
became exhausted, came to a bridge,
fell in the river and drowned.

But governments can't die.

In fact, we've set up a dedicated e-mail address:
www.tailtotooth@osd.pentagon.mil

Our assignment is not to try
to please everybody.

Some say it's like turning a battleship.
I suspect it's more difficult.

Well, fine, if there's to be a struggle,
so be it.

[*Applause.*]

There's a myth, sort of a legend,
that money
enters this building and disappears,
like a bright light
into a black hole,
never to be seen again.

This

This is not just about money.

In truth, there is a real person
at the other end of every dollar

Judas Horse

The domesticated Judas horse, trained to lead wild horses into a
pen, runs up front.

—Shannon Livick, "Wild Horses"

This time each year, I betray my kin.
Hardwired to herd, they go
where others follow. I lead them in.

But even wild horses believe in sin.
I've seen the way their eyes roll
back in fear. Still, I betray my kin

into that corral. Deceit's a thin
path beaten through my brain. So
what? They follow. I just lead them in.

I never question the flinty men
whose hands are looped with rope.
They say nothing as I betray my kin.

Liar, savior, traitor, friend:
take your pick. It makes no
difference when I lead them in.

An accusation twists inside the wind,
but nothing in my piebald hide will show
that every year, I betray my kin.
They always follow. So I lead them in.

Waiting with the Donkey

And Abraham said to his young men, "Stay here with the donkey; the
lad and I will go yonder and worship, and we will come back to you."

—Genesis 22:5

While you completed the Sunday crossword, icebergs wept themselves into the sea.
While you filled out your credit card application, a boy was born without a tongue.
While you ordered your coffee, the Library of Alexandria burned.

While you laughed, the carcinoma was growing.
While you kissed your wife, the last of something died off.
While you drank wine, the guillotine fell. And fell. And fell.

While you read by candlelight, a man in a faraway city laid mines in the road like
    an ellipsis . . .
While you admired the sun gone all syrupy, half of Europe caught the plague.
While you were eating breakfast (the egg a golden dome on its desert of toast),
    your prophet was put to death.

While you listened to your favorite song, the cell doors locked.
While you wept, we all wept.
While you wrote this poem, a bomb unwrapped an apartment building.

While you waited beside the donkey, a madman held up a knife, told his son to look
    the other way.

Reenactment of the Battle
for the Planet of the Apes

The old battlefield is a national park.
Tourists line the outer fences, taking pictures
to show to their relatives back home.
The reenactors of the Great Ape Regiment
wait on the hill, polishing their period-accurate
laser rifles, while in the old stream bed below,
Bravo Company pulls on their human masks,
tugging at the rubber cheeks until the eyeholes
line up just right. It's an honor to play
the doomed *Homo sapiens* troops,
who, in a few minutes, will go charging
up the hill, only to be cut down.

"We respect the humans' bravery,"
says the tour guide standing beside
the Statue of the Unknown Human Soldier,
"but evolution doesn't second-guess itself."

One boy's father buys him a plastic
human skull at the museum gift shop.

All the way home, the boy holds the skull,
runs a finger along the smooth crown
where the sagittal crest should be,
works the jaw up and down, as if
teaching the forgotten how to speak.

Wisconsin Poetry Series

Ronald Wallace, *Series Editor*

(B) = Winner of the Brittingham Prize in Poetry

(FP) = Winner of the Felix Pollak Prize in Poetry

(4L) = Winner of the Four Lakes Prize in Poetry